DAD JOKES

HOLIDAY EDITION!

YULE LOVE THEM!

JIMMY NIRO

sourcebooks

Published by Sourcebooks
P.O. Box 4410, Naperville, Illinois 60567-4410
(630) 961-3900
sourcebooks.com

Printed and bound in the United States of America.
VP 10 9 8 7 6 5 4 3

TABLE OF CONTENTS

INTRODUCTION

Dad jokes are back in this ho-ho-holiday edition! From the literal and ridiculous to the goofy and awkward, this book is sure to delight and embarrass your loved ones this holiday season. You'll find the merriest jokes on winter festivities, Hanukkah, Christmas, and New Year's, with the absolute best of the worst puns, stories, anti-jokes, and one-liners. Give the **gift** of **tear**able dad jokes **wrapped** up in good fun. Happy hollydays and a punny New Year!

SNOW WAY!
IT'S DAD JOKES!

I worked as a **snow**plow driver one winter. It was the **coolest** job I ever had.

Q: What is Jack Frost's favorite **drink**?
A: Fros**tea**.

There are always winners and **lugers** in the **Winter Olympics**.

Q: What did the **snowman** say to the snowwoman he was trying to woo?
A: "I only have **ice** for you."

········· ❄ ·········

I got addicted to **skiing** quickly. It was a **slippery slope**.

········· ❄ ·········

Q: What is Christopher **Walken**'s favorite Christmas carol?
A: "**Walken** in a Winter Wonderland."

········· ❄ ·········

Do **birds** know where they are going when they fly south for the winter, or do they just **wing** it?

········· ❄ ·········

Q: What is a snowman's greatest fear?
A: A blow-dryer.

I used to think **Frosty** the Snowman and I were good friends, but lately, he's been giving me the **cold** shoulder.

· ❄ ·

Q: What do you call an **iguana** in a snowstorm?
A: A b**lizzard**.

· ❄ ·

I'm so mad at you for making me skate on this **frozen lake**. You and I are on **thin ice**.

· ❄ ·

Q: Why did the **NSA whistle-blower** spend the whole winter in Russia?
A: He was **Snowden**.

· ❄ ·

Snowmen always get hurt when they play **sports**. They refuse to **warm up**.

Q: What happened to the **boxer** in the winter?
A: He was **out cold**.

· ❄ ·

I saw Frosty the Snowman out **shopping for carrots**. I guess you could say he was **picking his nose**.

· ❄ ·

Q: How did the **hipster** end up in the lake?
A: He went ice-skating before it was **cool**.

· ❄ ·

I heard **Humpty Dumpty** is having an awful winter, which is a shame, because he had a **great fall**!

· ❄ ·

Q: Why do bees stay in their hive all **winter**?
A: Swarm.

Winter is my favorite season. It's way **cooler** than summer.

....

"I can't believe it's going to snow today."

"But, Dad, it's eighty degrees outside!"

"That's why I can't believe it's going to snow."

....

I was clearing the snow off the driveway with my son today. He looked at me and said, "Dad, I wish you would just use a shovel."

....

Q: What do you call an elderly snowman?
A: Water

My wife was going out of town for work for a couple of days, and we had a bad winter storm forecast for our area. I mentioned to her that we should make a run to the grocery store before she left, in case one of us got stranded because of the snow. She rolled her eyes at me.

"You just want me to do the shopping because you're lazy," she said.

"No!" I replied. "I just want to make sure it's **snow** problem!"

❄

Q: Why did the **snowman** want a divorce?
A: Because he thought his spouse was a **flake.**

❄

Global warming is terrible for people who live in igloos. They'll have no privacy!

❄

Q: What did the **tree** say after a long winter?
A: "What a re**leaf**!"

My **snowman** threw a temper tantrum. I'm talking a complete **melt**down.

* * *

Q: What did the **hat** say to the **scarf**?
A: "You **hang around**. I'll go on a**head**."

* * *

"Dad, is it going to **snow** this Christmas?"

"I don't know. It's all up **in the air**."

* * *

Q: How did the snowman get to work?
A: **By icicle**.

* * *

Never go to a **wedding** in the winter. Someone always gets **cold feet**.

Q: What do you call a snowman's **prison**?
A: A **snow globe**.

--------------------------- ❄ ---------------------------

The **ski** trip started off great, but it was all **downhill** from there.

--------------------------- ❄ ---------------------------

Q: How does a penguin build a **house**?
A: **Igloos** it together.

--------------------------- ❄ ---------------------------

Everyone teased the snowman about his long and pointy **nose**. Luckily, he didn't **carrot** all.

--------------------------- ❄ ---------------------------

Q: What do you call a snowman's **cell phone**?
A: A snow**mobile**.

Snowmen can lose weight so easily. The pounds just **melt** away!

* * *

Q: How did the **polar bear** get so far from home?
A: He lost his **bear**ings.

* * *

A man was out with his friends for a day of skiing but was feeling a bit under the weather.

"Are you okay?" his buddy asked after the first run. "You look like you might be sick."

The man assured his friend that he was fine, and they got on the **chairlift** together to go back to the top of the hill. Something about the fresh air and the beautiful views on the chairlift made him feel better. By the time they got back up the mountain, he felt good as new.

He said, "Ahh, that was just the **lift** I needed!"

Q: Where's the best place to train **sled dogs**?

A: In the **mush** room.

.... ❄ ....

"Dad, my friend Jordan wears **snow pants** at recess."

"Wow. Why don't the teachers tell her to put pants on?"

.... ❄ ....

Q: What do you call a **disinterested** snowman?

A: A snow**board**.

.... ❄ ....

That **snow pun** was great. **Icy** what you did there.

.... ❄ ....

Q: Why did the skeleton stand out all night in the **snow**?

A: He was a **numb**skull.

I feel bad for **snowmen**. They can only smell **carrots**.

* * *

Q: What prize did the snowman's dog win at the **dog show**?
A: Best in snow.

* * *

Schools were closed today due to bad winter weather. It was literally too cool for school.

* * *

Q: Why couldn't the snowman get a tan?
A: Because snowmen have no melanin. Also, they melt in the sun.

* * *

"Dad, snow is **falling**!"

"I hope it doesn't get **hurt**."

Q: Where does Jack Frost keep his **money**?

A: In a snow**bank**.

You know it's cold outside when you walk outside and it's cold.

· · · · · · · · · · · · · · · · · · · ❄ · · · · · · · · · · · · · · · · · · ·

Q: How do you make an angry **snowman** calm down?
A: Tell him to take a **chill** pill.

· · · · · · · · · · · · · · · · · · · ❄ · · · · · · · · · · · · · · · · · · ·

One time, I sent my dad a **pile of snow** for Christmas. I called him a few hours later and asked him if he got my **drift**.

· · · · · · · · · · · · · · · · · · · ❄ · · · · · · · · · · · · · · · · · · ·

Q: What is a **snowman**'s favorite breakfast food?
A: **Frosted Flakes**.

· · · · · · · · · · · · · · · · · · · ❄ · · · · · · · · · · · · · · · · · · ·

Don't tell **jokes** when you're ice-skating. The ice might **crack up**.

At school, they announced our class was going on a winter field trip. When I got home that day, I asked my dad if he could sign the permission slip and give me some money for the excursion.

In response, he asked where we are headed and how much money I would need.

I told him, "We're going to the **ice rink** to skate. I only need five dollars to go."

My dad said, "Wow, now that's what I call a cheap **skate**!"

.... ❄ ....

"Dad, our snowman melted!"

"I think he's just dehydrated."

.... ❄ ....

Q: What do you call a snowman with a **six-pack**?
A: An **abdominal** snowman.

Q: What did the snowman say to the dog?

A: "Give me back my arms."

I was at work one morning after a snowstorm when I got a text from my mother.

"**Windows** frozen," it said. "Won't open."

I assumed she was talking about the windows in our basement, which did tend to freeze. I texted her back and said she could loosen them up by pouring lukewarm water on the edges and then tapping each edge gently with a hammer.

I got another text back a few minutes later and saw I'd misinterpreted.

It said, "Didn't work. **Computer** is completely broken now."

Q: What do you call a snowman **prom**?

A: A snow**ball**.

They told me we were going **sledding**, but we went skiing instead. I felt mi**sled**.

.... ❄ ....

Q: How do you find **Will Smith** in the snow?
A: Look for **fresh prints**.

.... ❄ ....

My **car** has been acting up all winter. I guess it's just being **salty**.

.... ❄ ....

That snowman looks **hungry**. Let's get him some ice**bergers**!

.... ❄ ....

Q: Why didn't **Guns N' Roses** make it to the winter gig?
A: Axl Froze.

"Dad, why don't you wear snow boots?"

"Because they will melt."

Q: What song did they sing at **Frosty the Snowman**'s birthday party?
A: "**Freeze** a Jolly Good Fellow."

Q: How do you make **anti**freeze?
A: Steal **her** blanket.

Q: Why do birds fly south for the winter?
A: It's too far to walk.

Q: What is **Jack Frost**'s favorite part of school?
A: Snow and tell.

·············· ❄ ··············

I'd love to get involved in winter **sports**, but I don't know where **toboggan**.

·············· ❄ ··············

Q: What do you get when you cross a snowman with a **vampire**?
A: Frost**bite**.

·············· ❄ ··············

I enjoy cold **weather**, but only to a certain **degree**.

·············· ❄ ··············

Q: What do **snowmen** do in their spare time?
A: They just **chill**.

HANUKKAH: IT'S LIT

It would be a Hanukkah miracle if we could all settle on one spelling of Chanukah.

·············· ··············

Q: What does someone say when they celebrate both Christmas and **Hanukkah**?
A: "Happy **challah**days!"

·············· ··············

I hope your holiday isn't drei**dull**.

"Dad, which hand is it better to light the menorah with?"

"Neither. It's best to light it with a candle."

Q: What would **Simba**, **Timon**, and **Pumbaa** say if they were Jewish?
A: "**Hanukkah matata**."

We were getting ready for a family Hanukkah party, and my mom asked me to pick up **chocolate coins** for the kids.

The store I went to didn't have any, so I bought regular chocolate bars instead.

My mom wasn't happy about this and begged me to go back to a different store instead. She said that regular chocolate wasn't the same and that the kids would be sad.

"I'm sick of your **gelt** trips, Mom!" I yelled at her.

Q: What's the **alpaca**'s favorite holiday?
A: **Llama**kah.

·· ❄ ··

My family loves to dance at our Hanukkah party. This year, we **Torah** the floor up.

·· ❄ ··

Q: What did the little **candle** say to the big candle?
A: "I'm **going out** tonight."

·· ❄ ··

"Dad, why can't we have a Hanukkah tree?"

"Because the last time we had a lighted bush, we spent forty years in the wilderness."

Kids, I just want to say
that I love you **a latke**.

Q: Why did the **dreidel** go to the doctor?
A: The room just kept **spinning**.

Sometimes I think **Christmas** and **Hanukkah** get too much attention. There should be **Kwanzaa**quences.

Two menorahs were sitting in the window. The first one said to the other, "Wow, it's really starting to get hot with all these candles."

Then the second one said, "Whoa, a talking menorah!"

Q: What holiday do **felines** celebrate?
A: Hanuk**cat**.

Q: What's the best thing to put into sufganiyot?
A: Your teeth.

My favorite part of Hanukkah is spinning the **dreidel**. That's just how I **roll**. I drop it like a **top**.

* * *

Q: How much Hanukkah gelt did the little **skunk** get?
A: One **scent**.

* * *

"Dad, where are all the cookies?"

"It was a Hanukkah miracle. I thought I only had one cookie, but somehow, I ate eight."

* * *

I got into work after Hanukkah, and my boss asked if something happened. She said I look **dreidel**ful.

Q: What did one **menorah** say to his valentine?

A: "You **light** me up."

································· ❄ ·································

My fiancé and I were driving the other day, and we passed by a bridge that was lit up with green and red lights for Christmas.

With a sigh, he turned to me and said, "It's always Christmas colors this season. They should've made the **bridge** blue and white for Hanukkah."

I turned to him and replied, "Sadly, Hanukkah always gets **passed over**."

································· ❄ ·································

Q: Who's a rabbi's favorite **rapper**?

A: Dr. Dreidel.

································· ❄ ·································

I saw a commercial on TV for a car that looked kind of like a **dreidel**, so I took it for a **spin**.

"Dad, I'm hungry. Will the latkes be long?"

"No, they'll be round."

One day, a woman went to the post office to buy stamps for her holiday cards.

She asked the worker at the service counter, "Can I please have fifty Hanukkah stamps?"

"What denomination?" the cashier asked.

Surprised and annoyed, the woman said, "Has it really come to this? Okay, I guess I'll take six Orthodox, twelve Conservative, and thirty-two Reform."

"Dad, why doesn't Mom like your **Hanukkah** puns?"

"Maybe she thinks I'm making **light** of the celebration."

SANTA SLEIGHS ALL DAY

Q: What is Santa's favorite **pizza**?
A: One that's **deep-pan**, **crisp**, and **even**.

"Dad, what nationality is Santa?"

"He's **Russian**."

"Really?"

"Yep. **Rushin'** to deliver all those presents!"

Q: What did they call Santa when he went **bankrupt**?

A: Saint **Nickel**-less.

· · · · · · · · · · · · · · · · · · · ❄ ·

Q: Why did Santa want to take a **music** class?

A: He was hoping to improve his w**rapping** skills.

· · · · · · · · · · · · · · · · · · · ❄ ·

A kid who doesn't believe in Santa is just a rebel without a Claus.

· · · · · · · · · · · · · · · · · · · ❄ ·

Q: Why does Santa hide out at the North Pole?

A: He's wanted for breaking and entering.

· · · · · · · · · · · · · · · · · · · ❄ ·

Q: How does Santa figure out who all the **naughty** kids are?

A: He has a **coal**ition.

"Dad, does Santa deliver presents to all the kids in the world without a **break**?"

"I would assume he takes a Santa **Pause** at some point."

Because of recent environmental regulations and the shockingly high price of coal, Santa decided to stop giving coal to naughty kids for Christmas. Instead, Santa decided that children should get stockings full of **chopped cabbage** and **mayonnaise**.

Santa refers to this new rule as "**Coal's Law**."

Q: What did the **dyslexic devil**-worshipper do?
A: He sold his soul to **Santa**.

Q: Why did Santa put a **clock** in his sleigh?
A: He wanted to see **time fly**.

Q: Why was Mrs. Claus mad at **Santa** when he got home on Christmas morning?
A: He smelled like **smoke**.

❄

If they ever pass a **law** that says you can't lie to your kids, I hope they include a Santa **clause**.

❄

Q: What do you call a Santa Claus who is **half human**, **half horse**?
A: A **Santaur**.

❄

Q: What kind of motorcycle does **Santa** ride?
A: A **Holly** Davidson.

❄

Every man goes through three stages: believing in Santa, not believing in Santa, and looking like Santa.

Q: Why is Santa really good at **grocery shopping**?

A: He makes a **list** and checks it twice.

· ❄ ·

Q: Why did **Santa** need to go see a therapist?

A: He didn't **believe** in himself.

· ❄ ·

Q: What's red and white, then red, then white, then red again?

A: Santa Claus rolling down a hill.

· ❄ ·

When Santa and his wife wanted to **split up**, they got a semicolon; they're great for separating **independent Claus**es.

· ❄ ·

Q: Why does Santa have three **gardens**?

A: So he can **hoe**, **hoe**, **hoe**.

Q: What defense **weapon** does Santa have on his sleigh, just in case he runs into trouble?
A: A **missile**toe.

· ❄ ·

Q: Where does Santa keep all his red **suits**?
A: In his Santa **Clauset**.

· ❄ ·

If you've seen one **Santa**, you've seen the **mall**.

· ❄ ·

Q: If Santa lives at the North Pole, where does the **East**er Bunny live?
A: The **East** Pole.

· ❄ ·

Q: What did Santa say when he ended up at the South Pole one Christmas?
A: "I'm a lost Claus."

Q: What nationality is Santa Claus?

A: North Polish.

Santa's great at racecar driving. He's always in the **pole** position.

· ❄ ·

One Christmas, Santa decided he was in need of a new **sleigh**. His old one was looking a little run-down and had lost a bit of speed over the years. He went to the nearest sleigh dealership and picked out a state-of-the-art new design.

When he went to pay, though, the salesperson refused him and said, "Oh no, sir. It's **on the house**."

· ❄ ·

Q: Why did Santa get a parking **ticket**?
A: He was parked in a s**no**w **parking** zone.

· ❄ ·

Q: What does **Christmas** have in common with a cat lost in the desert?
A: They both have **sandy claws**.

The great thing about Santa is that you can't see him, but you can feel his **presents**.

※

Q: How does Santa wash his hands before he eats?
A: Hand **Santa**tizer.

※

I love **Christmas**. Everyone gets **Santa**mental.

※

Q: What's **Santa**'s favorite kind of candy?
A: **Jolly** Ranchers.

※

Q: What do you get if Santa goes down the chimney when a **fire** is lit?
A: **Krisp** Kringle.

On the night before Christmas, I told my dad, "I'm worried about Santa."

He replied, "How come? It's Christmas!"

I asked, "Isn't it dangerous going into people's houses? What if something happens to him?"

My dad looked at me with a serious expression and said, "Don't worry. Santa knows karate."

I was really surprised to hear this and asked my dad how he knew that.

He responded, "Santa has a **black belt**!"

Q: What does Santa say when he's walking backward?
A: "Oh, oh, oh."

I've always been afraid of Santa Claus. My doctor said I was **Claus**trophobic.

Q: Why does Santa come down the **chimney**?

A: Because it **soot**s him.

.... ❄ ....

Q: What does Santa call his wife at **tax** time?

A: A **dependent** Claus.

.... ❄ ....

Q: Where does **Santa** stay when he takes his much-deserved post-Christmas vacation?

A: A **ho ho ho**tel.

.... ❄ ....

Q: Who brings presents to baby **sharks** at Christmastime?

A: Santa **Jaws**.

SANTA'S DEER LITTLE HELPERS

Christmas can be a stressful time of year. You really need to believe in your **elf**.

Q: What type of dinosaur is one of Santa's little helpers?

A: Ty**wrap**osaurus rex.

Q: What kind of car does an **elf** drive?

A: A **Toy**ota.

"Dad, the forecast says we will have **thunderstorms** tonight, but it's Christmas Eve! Will Santa be able to get here if it's raining?"

"Of course! Why do you think they call them **rein**deer?"

* * *

Q: Why did **Rudolph** get pulled over?
A: He ran a **red light**.

* * *

If Santa ever decides to fire the **elves**, I bet they would make great **short** order cooks.

* * *

Q: Why did the **reindeer** need dental work?
A: He had **buck** teeth.

Q: What do you call a **scary** reindeer?
A: A cari**boo**.

.... ❄ ....

Santa really only has two reindeer: Rudolph and Olive, the other reindeer.

.... ❄ ....

Q: What do you call an elf when she wins the **lottery**?
A: **Welfy**.

.... ❄ ....

Q: What do **reindeer** use to decorate their Christmas trees?
A: **Horn**aments.

.... ❄ ....

Flying in a **sleigh** sounds scary. I bet Santa just has to hold on for **deer** life.

"Dad, did you know that Santa and his **reindeer** are coming tonight?"

"Yeah, I **herd**."

Q: Why didn't **Santa** enroll his reindeer in public school?
A: They were **elf**-taught.

Q: What do you call a reindeer wearing earmuffs?
A: Anything you like; he can't hear you!

Did you ever hear about the **elf** who wanted to play professional basketball? I guess he didn't **measure** up.

Q: Who did Santa hire to play at the Christmas party for his **helpers**?

A: Elfis Presley.

One Christmas, when Santa was preparing to board his sleigh and head out for the night, he realized that he was missing one toy from his bag.

Frantically, he called over his most trusted **elf**, Buddy.

"Buddy, I need you to make me another toy," Santa said. "Do you think you can do that in ten minutes or less?"

"Don't worry, sir!" the elf exclaimed. "I'll make **short** work of it."

Q: Which reindeer is the best at **football**?

A: Blitzen.

Q: Why was Santa's **helper** so shy?

A: She had low **elf**-esteem.

Scrooge hates Christmas but loves reindeer. Every **buck** is deer to him.

·············· ❄ ··············

Q: How much does it **cost** to get Santa's sleigh to move?
A: Eight **bucks**.

·············· ❄ ··············

Q: Which of Santa's reindeer killed the **dinosaurs**?
A: Comet.

·············· ❄ ··············

I once heard an elf defending the shape of his **ears**, and I have to say, he made some good **points**.

·············· ❄ ··············

Q: What's the first thing Santa's elves learn in **school**?
A: The **elfabet**.

Did you hear about the **wiener dog** that helped pull Santa's sleigh this year? It was **dachshund** through the snow.

············· ❄ ·············

Q: Why was Santa disappointed in **Rudolph**'s report card?
A: He went **down in history**.

············· ❄ ·············

Q: What do you call **Santa**'s helpers?
A: Subordinate **Claus**es.

············· ❄ ·············

I've heard that **Rude**olph is really **impolite** to the other reindeer.

············· ❄ ·············

Q: Why do **Dasher** and **Dancer** love coffee?
A: Because they're Santa's star **bucks**.

Q: What's the first thing you should do when you visit **Comet**'s house?

A: Ring the **deer** bell.

.... ❄ ....

People act like the **North Pole** and the **South Pole** are exactly the same, but there's a whole **world of difference** between them.

.... ❄ ....

Q: What do you call a reindeer with no eyes?

A: I have no-eyed deer!

.... ❄ ....

Q: What happens to elves who land on the naughty list?

A: **Santa sack**s them.

Q: What do you call an **elf** with a music career?
A: A **wrap**per.

· ❄ ·

Q: What do you call a chicken at the North Pole?
A: Lost.

· ❄ ·

A Russian couple was walking down a street in Moscow when the husband felt a drop hit his nose.

"I think it's raining," he said to his wife.

"No, that feels like snow to me, dear," she replied.

Just then, a Communist Party official walked toward them. "Let's not fight about it," the man said to his wife. "Let's ask Comrade Rudolph whether it's officially raining or snowing."

"It's raining, of course," Comrade Rudolph said and walked on.

But the woman insisted, "I know that felt like snow."

The man quietly responded, "Rudolph the Red knows rain, dear."

DECK THE HALL-IDAYS

"Dad, why are you putting all the **ornaments** right next to each other?"

"Because they like **hanging** together!"

Q: What was the **bird**'s favorite Christmas story?
A: "How the **Finch** Stole Christmas."

I'm not sure if I like eggnog or not. I guess you could call me **eggnostic**.

Q: What did Adam say to Eve on the day before Christmas?
A: "It's Christmas, Eve!"

Q: What do you get when you cross a Christmas tree with an **iPhone**?
A: A pine**apple**.

"Dad, how do you feel about going on a **holiday** cruise?"

"Great, we can start at **Christmas Island** and go to **Easter Island**."

Q: Why are Christmas trees so bad at **knitting**?

A: Because they always drop their **needles**.

.... ❄ ....

Q: Why didn't the Christmas **turkey** eat dinner?

A: He was already **stuffed**.

.... ❄ ....

Mary and Joseph really got some curveballs thrown their way. It's a good thing they had such a **stable** marriage.

.... ❄ ....

Q: What did the **green beans** say to each other on Christmas?

A: "**Peas** on Earth."

.... ❄ ....

Q: How did the **angel** greet the shepherds?

A: He said "**halo**!"

"Dad, why don't you want a Christmas **tree** this year?"

"I can't trust them, Son. They seem kind of **shady**."

❄

Q: What happened to the man who stole an **advent calendar**?
A: He got **twenty-five days**.

❄

If you don't come to my Christmas party, **yule** be sorry!

❄

Q: Who is the Christmas **tree**'s favorite singer?
A: **Spruce** Springsteen.

Q: How did Scrooge win the **football** game?

A: The ghost of Christmas **passed**.

* * *

Have you seen our Christmas **tree** this year? It's **lit**!

* * *

Q: What did Mary say to the little drummer boy?

A: "No thanks, Jesus is sleeping."

* * *

Q: What did the doctor say to the **gingerbread** man?

A: "Try **icing** it."

* * *

"Would you like the eggnog in a bag, sir?"

"No, just leave it in the carton, please."

Q: What do you call a ghost that haunts your Christmas **tree**?

A: The ghost of Christmas **presents**.

.... ❄ ....

Christmas: or as I like to call it, the world's biggest baby shower.

.... ❄ ....

Q: Why was the Christmas tree green?

A: Most trees are green.

.... ❄ ....

Q: Who **hides** in a bakery at Christmas?

A: Mince **spies**.

.... ❄ ....

Q: How does the gingerbread man make his **bed**?

A: He starts with a cookie **sheet**.

My family and I were out shopping for Christmas dinner, buying supplies for all we would need to cook. As we were checking out, the cashier was trying to make small talk and asked what our plans were for the big meal.

"Oh, we're going to **smoke** a turkey for Christmas this year," I told him.

Eyeing our twenty-pound bird, he asked, "How do you fit that into a **pipe**?"

Q: Why was Mary mad at Joseph when they got to the inn in Bethlehem?
A: He forgot to make reservations.

"Dad, I don't want to wear an ugly sweater to the Christmas party."

"Well, we're all wearing them, **sweater** you like it or not."

Q: Why do people hang Christmas lights on their houses?
A: It's too dangerous to leave them lying on the driveway.

Ornaments get **addicted** to Christmas because they're **hooked on** trees their whole lives.

Q: What did the **sheep** say on Christmas?
A: "**Fleece** Navidad."

Q: What happened to the man who **decked** the halls?
A: He was charged with **assault**.

Fizz the season to celebrate! Let's **toast** with some **prosecc-ho**-ho-ho.

If your great-grandmother saw me making **mashed potatoes** out of a box, she would turn over in her **gravy**.

···················· ❄ ····················

Q: What does Ebenezer Scrooge call his **dog**?
A: Bah Hum-**Pug.**

···················· ❄ ····················

Q: What do you call an **ornament** when it's the only one on the Christmas tree?
A: The **Decoration** of Independence.

···················· ❄ ····················

"Dad, I love **Christmas**!"

"If you love it so much, why don't you **merry** it?"

I was talking with a guy at the Christmas tree lot, and he seemed a little **emotional**. But I guess you could say he works in a pretty **sappy** business.

Q: How should you serve **eggs Benedict** for a Christmas brunch?
A: There's no plate like chrome for the **hollandaise**.

I was helping my mom make Christmas dinner. She was doing all the hard work, and my only job was to keep an eye on the turkey.

Around the time dinner was supposed to be ready, she walked into the kitchen and asked, "How does the turkey **smell**?"

I gave the best response I could think of. "**Through its beak**, I'm guessing."

Q: What do you call a **cop** at a Christmas party?
A: Police Navidad.

· ❄ ·

Q: Why did the Christmas **cookie** go to the doctor?
A: He felt **merry crumby**.

· ❄ ·

I had the biggest Christmas tree this year. It was **tree**mendous.

· ❄ ·

Q: What's a **dog**'s favorite Christmas carol?
A: "**Bark**, the Herald Angels Sing."

· ❄ ·

Q: What color hair do **gingerbread** men have?
A: They're **bread**heads.

My family and I were on vacation for the holidays. One day, when I was heading down to the pool, I saw that there was some sort of event going on in the lobby. There were a bunch of chess masters sitting around, arrogantly bragging about their past games. When I got to the pool, my husband asked me what the event was.

I replied, "It's just a bunch of chess nuts boasting in an open foyer."

Q: What do you call Christmas at **Dwayne Johnson**'s house?
A: The Rock around the Christmas tree.

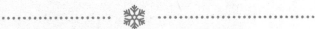

My daughter drew a few pictures of Christmas cookies that made me **laugh**. I guess you could call them **snicker** doodles.

Q: What do you call an **insect** that hates Christmas?
A: A hum**bug**.

.... ❄ ....

Q: What do you get if you eat Christmas **decorations**?
A: **Tinsel**itis.

.... ❄ ....

I love to sing Christmas carols to get in the holiday spirit. For me, this habit starts around Thanksgiving. My family really hates Christmas music but tolerates my incessant singing. This year, though, my wife was at the end of her rope.

"I'm sick of Christmas songs!" she yelled at me. "I'm going to kick you out of the house if you keep singing them."

I couldn't help myself, so I sang, "But, baby, it's cold outside!"

.... ❄ ....

Q: What's an **avocado**'s favorite Christmas song?
A: "**Guac**in' in a Winter Wonderland."

I like drinking **gin** around Christmas. It puts me in the holiday **spirit**.

· ❄ ·

Q: What is **Santa's** favorite thing to eat?
A: Falalafel.

· ❄ ·

Eggnog is okay I guess, but it's not all it's **cracked** up to be.

· ❄ ·

Q: What do you call a **boulder** decorated for Christmas?
A: A jingle bell **rock**.

· ❄ ·

Our neighbors have so many lights up, I can't tell if they're celebrating Christmas or the electric company!

Q: Who worked **on and off** over the holidays?
A: My Christmas **lights.**

Q: How did the **dinosaurs** celebrate Christmas?
A: They decorated the Christmas *T. rex*.

·· ❄ ··

Q: What did the **beaver** say to the Christmas tree?
A: "Nice **gnawing** you."

·· ❄ ··

I think we should buy a real Christmas **tree** this year. I just really feel like it would **spruce** things up.

·· ❄ ··

Q: What did **cumin** and **paprika** write on their Christmas card?
A: Christmas **thyme** is here! **Seasonings'** greetings.

·· ❄ ··

I wish I could keep my **advent calendar** forever, but its **days are numbered**.

Q: Who **trim**med the tree?
A: A **barber**.

. . . . ❄ . . . .

"Hey, Dad, Mom wants your help **fixing** Christmas dinner."

"Why? Is it **broken**?"

. . . . ❄ . . . .

I was going to serve **sweet potatoes** with Christmas dinner, but I sat on them, so now I'm serving **squash**.

. . . . ❄ . . . .

Q: What did **Bigfoot** keep asking his parents in December?
A: Is it Christmas **yeti**?

Q: What's the **forty-fourth president**'s favorite Christmas song?

A: "**Barack**in' Around the Christmas Tree."

I've been collecting **candy canes** for years. They're all in **mint** condition.

"How much did Jesus **weigh** when he was born?"

"I don't think Mary and Joseph had a way to find that out, Dad."

"But the song says 'a **weigh** in the manger'!"

THE GIFT OF A GOOD PUN

Christmas is the **present** holiday.

Q: Why did Captain Nemo get **coal** for Christmas?
A: He was on the *Nautil*us.

My **superpower** is that I can see inside wrapped presents. It's a **gift**.

"Dad, for Christmas this year, can I have a **camera**?"

"I'm not sure I like that idea. You'll **shoot** your eye out!"

My wife and daughter both got me **bow ties** for Christmas and asked me which one I liked better. I tried to choose, but it was a **tie**.

Q: What did one **sheep** tell another it wanted as a gift?
A: "All I want for Christmas is **ewe**."

Leonardo da **Grinch**i stole presents on Christmas. I guess you could say he was a **con** artist.

A dad was out Christmas shopping for his son. He was looking for a **Terminator** action figure, because his son loved Arnold Schwarzenegger movies.

At the toy store, the dad was having trouble finding what he wanted, so he approached an employee.

He said, "Excuse me, do you know where I can find Terminator action figures?"

The toy store employee looked at him and then pointed toward the back of the store.

"**Aisle B, back**."

Q: What did the naughty **soccer** announcer get for Christmas?
A: COOOOOAAAALLLLLLLL!

My kids just toss wrapping paper **everywhere** when they open presents. It's a Christ**mess**.

Q: What did the bald man say when he received a **comb** for Christmas?

A: "I'll never **part** with it."

·········· ❄ ··········

I got some new **mittens** for Christmas. They fit like a **glove**.

·········· ❄ ··········

"Dad, can I have a puppy for Christmas?"

"What? No! You'll have turkey like everyone else."

·········· ❄ ··········

My **great**-grandfather always got me great gifts for Christmas. My **so-so** grandmother got me socks.

Q: How did **Santa** get invited to the wedding?

A: His **presents** was requested.

.... ❄ ....

I ran out of paper while I was **wrapping presents** and I didn't know what to do about it. I just couldn't **wrap** my head around it.

.... ❄ ....

One year for Christmas, my mother-in-law gave me a sweater that she had knitted.

"I love it!" I said. "I'll be sure to wear it the next time we see you."

True to my word, when my mother-in-law invited us to a party a few days later, I wore the sweater. When we walked through the door, my mother-in-law took one look at me and burst into tears.

"What's her problem?" I asked my wife.

It turns out it was an ugly sweater party.

I got my wife a basket of **fragrances** for Christmas.
The gift just made a lot of **scents**.

Q: What did the pirate get for Christmas?
A: A peg **leg**, but it wasn't his main present, just a
stocking stuffer.

For Christmas, I got you a **gift card**. Try not to
spend it all in **one place**.

I hear Christmas trees love the **past**. You could say
that the **presents** beneath them.

Q: Why didn't Santa have any presents for the **rope**?
A: It was too **knot**ty.

"Dad, why is Mom mad at you?"

"Well, she asked me to get her **diamonds** for Christmas, and I guess I misunderstood the request."

"What did you get her?"

"A **deck of cards**."

Do you want to hear a joke about Christmas and wrapping **paper**? Never mind. It's **tear**able.

I got a new sweater for Christmas, but it was full of **static electricity**. When I returned it to the store, they were **shocked**.

One Christmas morning, I got a really confusing text from my dad.

The message read, "Heo, Son! Have a hoy joy Christmas! Your mom iked her gifts. Thanks for heping me pick them out for her! Et's get together for dinner soon."

The next day when I met my dad for dinner, I had to ask, "Dad, what was the deal with that text? Is your phone broken or something?"

He laughed and then said one word: "**Noel**!"

⁂

I got you a snowman for Christmas. Some assembly required.

⁂

"Dad, are you all finished with your **Christmas shopping** yet?"

"I'm just **wrapping** things up."

I got a **reversible** jacket for Christmas! I can't wait to see how it **turns out**.

.... ❄️ ....

Q: What did the third **king** say after the other two had presented their gifts to baby Jesus?
A: "But wait—there's **myrrh**."

.... ❄️ ....

I got a **universal** remote for Christmas. This changes **everything**!

.... ❄️ ....

Q: Why is a **broken drum** one of the best Christmas presents that you can give and receive?
A: Because you **can't beat** it.

.... ❄️ ....

If I asked for **matador** equipment for Christmas, would that be a big **red flag**?

NEW YEAR, NEW JOKES

A New Year's **resolution** is something that goes in **one year** and out the other.

Q: What is **corn**'s favorite holiday?
A: New **Ear**'s Day.

Happy New Year! Wow, I remember last year like **it was yesterday**.

Every year, when it's almost midnight on New Year's Eve, my dad gets up in the middle of the room and raises his left leg. He will hold it there until the clock strikes twelve.

When we ask him what he's doing, he says, "I just want to start the New Year off on the right foot!"

I'm always the chattiest at **New Year's Eve** parties. Something about the holiday really gives me a **bubbly** personality.

Q: What did Steven like to be called on New Year's Day?
A: New Year's Steve.

When **Dracula** passed out on New Year's Eve, there was a **count**down.

When I was growing up, my dad loved to tell bad jokes. It was especially common for him to tell them around the holidays, when lots of people were around to be his audience.

One year, at about 11:55 p.m. on New Year's Eve, my mom was getting irritated with him and asked him to lay off the jokes for a bit.

My dad looked remorseful and apologized to her and the rest of us.

He said, "Okay, I promise not to make any bad jokes for the rest of the year."

Q: How do you know you've **found** the New Year's Eve party?
A: Look for the "Auld Lang **Sign**."

I'm not impressed with the organizers of the New Year's Eve celebration at **Times Square**. They always **drop the ball**.

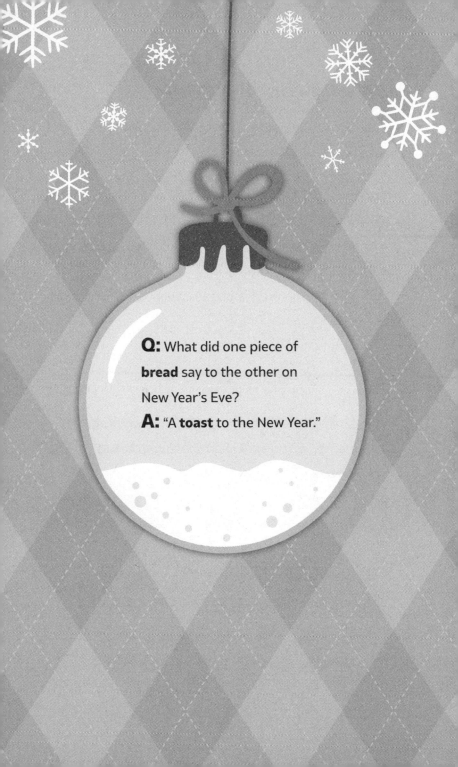

Q: What did one piece of **bread** say to the other on New Year's Eve?

A: "A **toast** to the New Year."

My New Year's **resolution** is **1080p**.

* * *

Last New Year's Eve, my dad was getting hungry around 11:30 p.m., so he ordered a pizza for delivery. The delivery driver showed up around forty-five minutes later, and my dad gave him an incredulous look.

He said, "I ordered this pizza last year and I'm just getting it now?"

* * *

I love Christmas, but New Year's Eve is **stressful** for me. My doctor said I had something called "Auld L**anxiety**."

* * *

Q: When is a dad hungriest?
A: New Year's morning. He hasn't eaten all year!

I always make a New Year's resolution about **Velcro**. That way, at least one of my resolutions **sticks**.

.... ❄ ....

Q: What do **vampires** sing on New Year's Eve?
A: "Auld **Fang** Syne."

.... ❄ ....

Q: Why did the couple get **married** at midnight on December 31?
A: They wanted to **ring** in the New Year.

.... ❄ ....

"Dad, what are we doing for New Year's Eve this year?"

"Not sure yet. I thought we'd play it by **year**."

You should never tell someone you love them on **January 1**. It's only the **first date**!

Q: What do you say to a **cat** on December 31?
A: "Happy **Mew** Year!"

"Dad, why are you showering again this morning? You just showered last night before the New Year's Eve party."

"Because I haven't showered since last year!"

Celebrating the New Year has a lot of **pros**, but the biggest downside is the **con**fetti.